A New True Book

KOALAS

By Emilie U. Lepthien

◑P CHILDRENS PRESS ®
CHICAGO

PHOTO CREDITS

© Cameramann International Ltd.—7, 12, 17 (left)

© Virginia Grimes—17 (top right), 44 (left)

H. Armstrong Roberts—© Photo Media, 28-29; C. Zefa, 33

© Emilie Lepthien—17 (bottom right)

Photri—13, 38 (right); © Fritz Prenzel, 2, 24

Root Resources—© Louise K. Broman, 6

© San Diego Zoo—42; © Val Thompson, 30 (left); © Ron Garrison, 43, 44 (right)

Shostal Associates/SuperStock International, Inc.—26 (bottom), 37

Tom Stack & Associates—© John Cancalosi, 4, 26 (top right), 31, 32 (left)

© Lynn M. Stone—14, 16, 20, 22 (2 photos), 34, 36, 45

SuperStock International, Inc.—Cover, 9, 10

TSW-Click/Chicago—© Dallas & John Heaton, 15

Valan—© Tom W. Parkin, 18; © John Cancalosi, 26 (top left), 27 (2 photos), 30 (right), 32 (right), 38 (left), 39, © A. B. Joyce, 41

Cover: Koala with baby on her back

A koala mother and baby

To my former co-workers, the faculty and staff of Wicker Park Elementary School and Upper Grade Center, Chicago

Library of Congress Cataloging-in-Publication Data

Lepthien, Emilie U. (Emilie Utteg)
  Koalas / by Emilie U. Lepthien.
    p.   cm. — (A New true book)
  Includes index.
  Summary: Describes the characteristics and behavior of the marsupial whose name means "one who doesn't drink."
  IBSN 0-516-01108-1
  [1. Koala.] I. Title. [DNLM: 1. Koala—Juvenile literature.]
QL737.M384L47   1990
599.2—dc20   90-2219
                                        CIP
                                        AC

TABLE OF CONTENTS

KOALAS ARE MAMMALS

Koalas are Australian mammals. They are small furry creatures that like to curl up in eucalyptus trees. They sleep for most of the day and are active in the evening.

When they are awake, koalas usually sit upright. They hold their heads up and look sleepily at the world with their yellowish-brown button eyes.

The aborigines of Australia

called this animal *koala*, which means "one who doesn't drink." Koalas get almost all the water they need from the eucalyptus leaves they eat. About two-thirds of the tender eucalyptus leaves consist of water and often there is dew on the leaves.

Koalas eat the leaves and buds of evergreen eucalyptus trees.

AUSTRALIAN NATIVES

Koalas are found in eastern Australia. They live in the great eucalyptus forests in Queensland and New South Wales. Koalas have plenty to eat. No other animal in the forest eats eucalyptus.

Queensland koalas weigh about twenty pounds and grow to be two feet tall. The koalas in Victoria and New South Wales are a bit bigger, but they are the same species.

Koalas spend most of their lives in eucalyptus trees. They come down to the ground only when they move from one tree to another. Sometimes they leap from tree to tree to find more food.

FUR COATS

Koalas have thick gray or brown fur. The outer coat is made up of guard hairs, which grow close together. Underneath, there is a coat of short soft fur. This double coat keeps koalas warm.

Their thick fur makes koalas look much fatter than they really are. Their belly fur is not as thick and it is much lighter in color.

A koala prepares for bad weather.

In harsh weather, koalas curl up in a ball with their backs to the rain and the wind. Their fur coats keep them warm and dry.

The koala's large ears help it to hear well.

Koala ears are large and furry. Their hearing is very good.

Koalas can be noisy. They grunt and growl and make clicking noises. When they are hurt, they sound almost like human babies crying.

SPECIAL FEET, SPECIAL LEGS

Koalas have five toes on each foot. Each front foot— or paw—has two toes that work like thumbs. They help the animals pick leaves and grip tree branches. They also help koalas climb.

The koala has two "thumbs" on each front paw.

Each hind foot has one
thumblike toe. The other
toes have sharp claws.
Koalas use their claws to
groom their fur. They can
also use them for defense.

Koalas are
good climbers.

Their front legs are long
and help them climb. They
reach up the tree trunk and
hold on tightly. Then, with
their short hind legs, they
push themselves up. When
they find a comfortable fork

Koalas sleep eighteen
to twenty hours a day.

in the tree, they curl up and
fall asleep.

Although their legs are
not well adapted for running,
koalas can move quickly on
the ground.

The koala has no tail.

17

SPECIAL SENSES

Their curved, black noses
are large and shiny. Koalas
have a very good sense of
smell. At certain times, some
kinds of eucalyptus leaves

are poisonous. Koalas can smell this poisonous acid and do not eat those leaves.

They can also smell the scent that a male koala uses to mark a tree as his territory. The scent comes from a musk gland on the male's chest. The male who marks the tree defends his territory if another male tries to climb the tree.

Koalas need
sharp teeth
to cut and
chew the
eucalyptus.

SPECIAL FOOD

Koalas have very sharp
teeth. They have eight teeth
for cutting, two for ripping
the leaves off, and twenty for
chewing and grinding the
leaves and bark.

They store leaves in their cheek pouches like sqirrels until they are ready to eat them.

Although there are hundreds of varieties of eucalyptus, most koalas eat only about thirty-five kinds. But some koalas are even choosier and eat only two or three kinds.

They love to eat the base of tender leaves, which may contain more sugar. The cyanide found in eucalyptus leaves may cause them to be drowsy most of the time. Koalas sleep eighteen to twenty hours a day.

A koala eats more than two pounds of leaves a day. Eucalyptus leaves are mostly

Koalas spend a lot of time eating when they are awake.

fiber. There is very little nourishment in them. It takes almost three days for the leaves to be digested. The eucalyptus makes the koalas smell like cough drops.

Sometimes koalas eat soil. The soil contains needed minerals that the koalas do not get from the leaves.

KOALAS ARE MARSUPIALS

Although koalas look like teddy bears, they are not related to bears at all. Koalas are marsupials— animals that carry their young in a pouch on the mother's belly.

The koala (above left), the kangaroo (above right), and the wallaby (below) are all marsupials. The mothers carry their babies in a pouch.

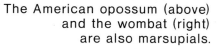
The American opossum (above)
and the wombat (right)
are also marsupials.

There are many
marsupials in Australia,
including kangaroos,
wombats, and wallabies. The
opossums found in North
America and South America
are also marsupials.

27

KOALA PARENTS

Koalas live singly or in small groups. A male may have a harem of several females.

When a female is ready to

mate, she often stops eating.
She grunts and bellows. Her
future mate also bellows.
Mating usually occurs in
December, which is
summertime in Australia.

KOALA CUBS

About a month after the pair has mated, a tiny cub is born. It is only three-fourths of an inch long and weighs about half a gram. The tiny cub cannot see. It is pink and hairless.

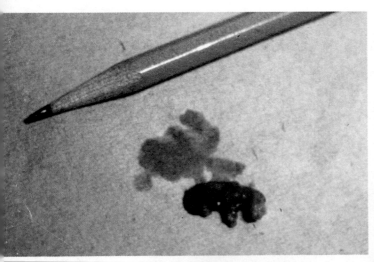

The tiny newborn koala seen above will leave its mother's pouch in about six months. Then the baby clings to its mother's chest (right).

It finds its way up into the pouch and feeds on its mother's milk.

For five to six months it stays in the pouch. At last, the cub climbs out of the pouch and clings to the fur on its mother's chest. At first, it stays out of the pouch only a very short time.

At six months, the koala
cub still depends on its
mother for food and protection.

When the cub is six
months old, the mother koala
begins to feed it with partly
digested leaves called pap.
Each day the cub stays

An older cub
rides on its
mother's back.

out of the pouch a little
longer. Finally, the mother
pushes the cub onto her
back. It still feeds partly on
its mother's milk and pap.
But it also nibbles some
small leaves. It will soon be
a year old.

Even when the cub is almost as big as its mother and has its fur coat, it rides on her back. It still likes to be held by its mother like a human baby. Perhaps it feels safer there than on her back.

Male koalas do not help their mates with the cubs. Although they may live in the same tree, males ignore their offspring.

Koala mother with an older cub.

Even when its mother
mates again, the cub stays
close to her. When the cub
is two years old, an adult
male—perhaps its own

father—drives it away. By
that time, the cub is old
enough to find its own trees.
When it is four years old, it
will be ready to mate, too.

A THREATENED SPECIES

Koalas have few natural enemies. Only *dingos* (wild dogs), owls, and some lizards may attack a small cub that strays away from its mother. Humans are the koala's worst enemy.

Young koalas are defenseless. They have few natural enemies besides the dingo (below).

For the first thirty years of
the twentieth century, koalas
were hunted for their fur.
They were in danger. In 1924

alone, over two million skins were exported.

Today, koalas are protected in Australia. Hunting koalas has been forbidden since the early 1930s. The koalas are no longer an endangered species. But still their existence is threatened. Some of their natural habitat

A eucalyptus forest in Australia

is being destroyed. The eucalyptus forests are cut down because people need more land for houses and farming.

Koalas from Queensland arrived at the San Diego Zoo in 1976

NEW BREEDING PROGRAMS

In 1976, Australia sent six young koalas to the United States in honor of America's bicentennial.

A koala
baby gets
weighed at the
San Diego Zoo.

A breeding program
began in the San Diego Zoo.
In the next thirteen years,
forty cubs were born. Now
some koalas are on loan to

other zoos and animal parks for breeding purposes. Most of the koalas live in zoos where eucalyptus trees grow. Otherwise, the zoo must get a fresh supply of leaves regularly.

Computers keep track of the zoo koalas. Scientists do

A zoo koala dines on eucalyptus leaves while a scientist keeps track of its family tree on a computer.

not want koalas that are
related to mate. They want
to avoid inbreeding, so that
the koala cubs will be strong
and healthy.

WORDS YOU SHOULD KNOW

aborigines (ab • or • RIJ • in • eez) — the people who were the first to live in a place, especially the first people of Australia

acid (ASID) — a sour-tasting chemical

adapted (uh • DAP • ted) — changed to fit new conditions, such as a different climate

Australian (awss • TRAIL • yan) — of Australia, a continent in the western South Pacific Ocean

bicentennial (by • sen • TEN • ee • yal) — happening once in two hundred years; a two-hundred-year anniversary

cyanide (SY • en • ide) — a poisonous chemical

digest (dih • JEST) — to change food in the stomach and intestines so that the body can use it

dingo (DING • oh) — a wild dog found in Australia

endangered (en • DAIN • jerd) — in danger of dying out

eucalyptus (yoo • kuh • LIP • tis) — a type of tall tree with broad, evergreen leaves

fiber (FYE • ber) — tough, stringy plant parts that are not digested

fork (FORK) — the point where a tree divides into branches

groom (GROOM) — to clean and make neat

guard hairs (GARD HAIRZ) — long hairs in the outer fur of animals

habitat (HAB • ih • tat) — the place where an animal usually is found

inbreeding (IN • bree • ding) — breeding with animals that are closely related

kangaroo (kang • uh • ROO) — an animal of Australia that has small front legs and large, powerful back legs; the female carries her young in a pouch

mammal (MAM • il) — one of a group of warm-blooded animals that have hair and nurse their young with milk

marsupial (mar • SOO • pee • il) — an animal whose babies are carried by the female in a pouch on the front of her body

mineral (MIN • er • il) — substance such as iron or calcium that is needed by the body in small amounts

musk gland (MUSK GLAND) — a small sac under the skin that produces a substance with a strong and lasting odor

nourishment (NER • ish • mint) — substances in food that produce growth and health

opossum (oh • PAHSS • um) — a small marsupial that lives mostly in trees

poisonous (POY • zun • niss) — containing poison; causing sickness or death if eaten

species (SPEE • ceez) — a group of related plants or animals that are able to interbreed

territory (TAIR • ih • tor • ee) — an area with definite boundaries that an animal lives in

wallaby (WAWL • uh • bee) — an Australian animal that is like a kangaroo but is much smaller

wombat (WAHM • bat) — an Australian marsupial that burrows in the ground; it looks like a small bear

INDEX

About the Author

*Emilie Utteg Lepthien earned a BS and MA Degree and certificate
in school administration from Northwestern University. She taught
third grade, upper grade science and social studies, was a
supervisor and principal of Wicker Park School for twenty years.
Mrs. Lepthien has also written and narrated science and social
studies scripts for the Radio Council (WBEZ) of the Chicago Board
of Education.*

*Mrs. Lepthien was awarded the American Educator's Medal by
Freedoms Foundation. She is a member of Delta Kappa Gamma
Society International, Illinois Women's Press Association, National
Federation of Press Women, Iota Sigma Epsilon Journalism
sorority, Chicago Principals Association, and active in church
work. She has co-authored primary social studies books for Rand,
McNally and Company and served as educational consultant for
Encyclopaedia Britannica Films.*